# She Persisted

## KALPANA CHAWLA

— INSPIRED BY —

# She Persisted

by Chelsea Clinton & Alexandra Boiger

· · · · · · · · · · · · · · · · · · · · · · · · · · · · · · · · · · · · · · · ·

# KALPANA CHAWLA

· · · · · · · · · · · · · · · · · · · · · · · · · · · · · · · · · · · · · · · ·

*Written by*
## Raakhee Mirchandani

*Interior illustrations by*
## Gillian Flint

**PHILOMEL**

PHILOMEL BOOKS
An imprint of Penguin Random House LLC, New York

First published in the United States of America by Philomel Books,
an imprint of Penguin Random House LLC, 2023

Text copyright © 2023 by Chelsea Clinton
Illustrations copyright © 2023 by Alexandra Boiger

Philomel Books is a registered trademark of Penguin Random House LLC.

Visit us online at PenguinRandomHouse.com.

Library of Congress Cataloging-in-Publication Data is available.

Printed in the United States of America

HC ISBN 9780593620632
PB ISBN 9780593620649

1st Printing

LSCC

Edited by Talia Benamy and Jill Santopolo.
Design by Ellice M. Lee.
Text set in LTC Kennerley Pro.

Dear Reader,

As Sally Ride and Marian Wright Edelman both powerfully said, "You can't be what you can't see." When Sally said that, she meant that it was hard to dream of being an astronaut, like she was, or a doctor or an athlete or anything at all if you didn't see someone like you who already had lived that dream. She especially was talking about seeing women in jobs that historically were held by men.

I wrote the first *She Persisted* and the books that came after it because I wanted young girls—and children of all genders—to see women who worked hard to live their dreams. And I wanted all of us to see examples of persistence in the face of different challenges to help inspire us in our own lives.

I'm so thrilled now to partner with a sisterhood of writers to bring longer, more in-depth versions of these stories of women's persistence and achievement to readers. I hope you enjoy these chapter books as much as I do and find them inspiring and empowering.

And remember: If anyone ever tells you no, if anyone ever says your voice isn't important or your dreams are too big, remember these women. They persisted and so should you.

Warmly,

*Chelsea Clinton*

# She Persisted

She Persisted: TEMPLE GRANDIN

She Persisted: DEB HAALAND

She Persisted: BETHANY HAMILTON

She Persisted: DOROTHY HEIGHT

She Persisted: FLORENCE GRIFFITH JOYNER

She Persisted: HELEN KELLER

She Persisted: CORETTA SCOTT KING

She Persisted: CLARA LEMLICH

She Persisted: RACHEL LEVINE

She Persisted: MAYA LIN

She Persisted: WANGARI MAATHAI

She Persisted: WILMA MANKILLER

She Persisted: PATSY MINK

She Persisted: FLORENCE NIGHTINGALE

She Persisted: SALLY RIDE

She Persisted: MARGARET CHASE SMITH

She Persisted: SONIA SOTOMAYOR

She Persisted: MARIA TALLCHIEF

She Persisted: DIANA TAURASI

She Persisted: HARRIET TUBMAN

She Persisted: OPRAH WINFREY

She Persisted: MALALA YOUSAFZAI

# KALPANA
# CHAWLA

# TABLE OF CONTENTS

............................................................

# Punjab Dreams

K alpana Chawla was a celebrated NASA astronaut and the first Indian American woman to go to space. But before orbiting Earth, little Kalpana loved making paper airplanes and watching planes fly overhead from the roof of her home in India.

She was born on March 17, 1962, in Karnal, a town in the state of Haryana in India. Her mother, Sanjyothi, and her father, Banarasi Lal, lovingly called her Montu, a sweet nickname. She had two older sisters, Sunita and Deepa, and a big brother named Sanjay. And it wasn't until Montu was three years old and ready to go to school that she needed a "real" name, which she had never had before. She chose the name Kalpana herself.

Kalpana means *imagination* in Hindi, one of the languages her family spoke. It was the perfect name for this smart, brave, and fearless Indian girl who spent many nights on the roof, sometimes sleeping on a charpai, a traditional woven bed, imagining herself flying through the sky.

Her whole family knew about her passion for flight and airplanes. Years later, Kalpana's mom remembered her asking about the sun and the moon, eager to know more about what she saw

in the sky. Her dad remembered Kalpana asking how planes worked. Her natural curiosity and questions were clues for her parents and teachers: Kalpana was exceptional.

Karnal was a small town, but it had both an airport and a flying club, which is an organization that provides members with access to planes. Kalpana was lucky to live there. She often saw Pushpak airplanes, a type of Indian plane, and gliders in the sky above her hometown. She and Sanjay would ride their bikes to the Karnal airport to watch the small aircrafts take off and land. Once, her dad organized a plane ride for Kalpana to see Karnal from up in the sky. This was Kalpana's first time in the air. When she landed back on the ground, she couldn't stop tapping her foot with excitement. She loved flying.

A hardworking and dedicated student, Kalpana made her mark and excelled in every classroom she sat in. When it was time to graduate, she set her sights on her next goal. Kalpana wanted to study aeronautical engineering, a field related to aircraft and spacecraft. It wasn't common for women to study engineering at that time, but Kalpana persisted, applying to Punjab Engineering College in Chandigarh, a couple of hours from her family home.

But after her interview, she was told that women don't major in aeronautical engineering and that she should try mechanical engineering instead. Someone at the college even tried to get her to change her mind about joining the engineering program at all. But Kalpana knew what she wanted to do. In 1978, she became the first

woman to ever enroll in the school's aeronautical engineering program. There wasn't even a girls' dorm for her to stay in! Kalpana was determined to chase her dreams, and nothing—and no one—was going to stop her.

Her room in the apartment she rented in Chandigarh was covered in images of airplanes, astronauts, and space shuttles. There was no denying her passion! Dr. S. C. Sharma, one of Kalpana's college professors, later noted that Kalpana was the kind of student who always sat in the front of the classroom. She wasn't afraid to ask questions, raising her hand high and making sure her voice was heard. The whole class benefited from having a smart, thoughtful person like Kalpana among them, pushing them all to be better students.

Her time there went quickly, and in the

summer of 1982, Kalpana graduated. She made history as the first woman to graduate from the school with a degree in aeronautical engineering, but that wasn't enough for her. Kalpana had her sights set on her next big goal: applying and being accepted to a master's degree program in the United States of America.

# CHAPTER 2

# Texas Dreams

When Kalpana was accepted to three American universities, her father wasn't too excited about his daughter moving across the seas, far away from her home. But it was time for Kalpana to spread her wings. She wanted to keep studying aeronautical engineering, and, in 1982, she decided to move to Arlington, Texas, and attend the University of Texas.

The university was thrilled to have a brilliant

mind like Kalpana in their program. They even offered her an assistantship! That meant that Kalpana had to work twenty hours a week, on top of all the hours she spent studying, but it also helped her pay for school. It was uncommon for a foreign student to receive this offer, but the school thought she was outstanding. While helpful, the assistantship also meant that Kalpana, now twenty years old, had to hustle harder than many other students. But Kalpana never shied away from hard work.

"I came to America because it's the best place in the world for aviation. It's that simple," Kalpana said about her decision to move. America was fortunate to have an immigrant woman like Kalpana Chawla on her shores.

Life in Texas was different from Karnal and

Chandigarh. Luckily for Kalpana, though, she made a good friend soon after she moved into her apartment building. That neighbor, Jean-Pierre Harrison, would later become her husband. He was a twenty-five-year-old British American man training to become a professional pilot. "I was immediately struck by the inner fire that glowed through her beautiful dark eyes," Jean-Pierre later wrote about the first time he met his future wife.

The two bonded over their shared excitement for aviation, and they also enjoyed hiking, swimming, and scuba diving together. In 1983, Kalpana and Jean-Pierre got married. Some young women where she was from didn't have the freedom to choose their spouses or travel abroad for studies. But Kalpana wasn't going to be grounded by customs she didn't agree with. She was in

charge of her own future, and nothing was going to stop her.

In 1984, after getting her master's degree, Kalpana enrolled at the University of Colorado Boulder. She wasn't done learning, and this time, she was going to get her PhD, which is the most advanced degree you can get from a university.

Kalpana enjoyed being outdoors in nature, hiking, skiing, snowshoeing, and tubing. Always interested in how things worked, Kalpana decided to try a science experiment of her own one day while out on a wintry walk. Curious about touching cold metal with her tongue, something she had been warned not to do, Kalpana touched the tip of her tongue to a railing. This might not have been her best idea, because it's possible that her tongue could have gotten stuck to the railing. She was lucky to be able to free herself without a severe injury, though, and she never tried that again!

Kalpana enjoyed visiting Jefferson County International Airport and Boulder Municipal Airport at night, watching the stars and planes. After years of dreaming about flying lessons since she was little Montu, she finally started them. She got her private pilot's license for single-engine land airplanes and began taking glider lessons. Kalpana's dreams were taking flight.

She started wondering what it would be like to apply to NASA Astronaut Corps. To be an American astronaut, though, you need to be an American citizen, and Kalpana was in the United States on a student visa. Guided by her dreams of space travel, Kalpana started the process

for permanent residency and then American citizenship.

In 1988, Kalpana Chawla graduated and earned her PhD. She was headed for big, world-changing things. But first, she was off to Sunny-vale, California, to the NASA Ames Research Center, where she would be starting a job as a research scientist. It was her first job at NASA, but it wouldn't be her last.

# California Dreams

The Palo Alto flying club became Kalpana's new flight school. She started training and eventually earned her commercial pilot's license, and her husband joined the club as a flight instructor. Kalpana loved to fly whenever she could, even taking short trips during her lunchtime, and, together with a small group of other woman pilots, some longer day trips as well. She was only a bit over five feet tall, which made flying a bit difficult—it was sometimes hard to reach the plane's rudder pedals! But Kalpana used her problem-solving skills and innovative mind and glued thick rubber soles to the bottoms of her shoes. After that, reaching the pedals was no problem.

Always interested in learning new things, Kalpana also joined the Abhinaya Dance Company in nearby San Jose to train in a classical Indian dance called Bharatanatyam. She also stayed connected to her Indian roots by attending Odissi, Kathak, and Bharatanatyam dance performances and South Asian musical concerts. Her home and family in India never lost their special place in her heart, and she went back to visit them when she could, though not as often as she would have liked.

Kalpana became a US citizen on April 10,

1991, completing her immigration to America. Immigrants are people who live permanently in a foreign country. She had mixed feelings about giving up her Indian citizenship, but she couldn't be both a citizen of India and the US. And even though she was supposed to return her Indian passport, which would no longer work to help her get into the country, she decided to keep it. Kalpana Chawla was officially an American, but she knew that immigrants were also made up of the countries they had come from and that India would be a part of her forever.

Once, when Kalpana was asked about her Indian American identity after she first launched into space, she said: "On one of the night passes, I dimmed the lights in the flight deck and saw the stars. When you look at the stars and the galaxy, you feel that you are not just from any particular piece of land but from the solar system. I could extend the whole thing—maybe one day people will go to other galaxies, and then what would we say? Where did we come from? 'I am a resident of the Milky Way'?" She was glad to be a citizen of our solar system.

By 1993, Kalpana was the vice president of Overset Methods, Inc., a company that she started with three of her NASA Ames colleagues. They did similar work to what they had been doing at NASA, but this time, they were their own bosses. Kalpana's rise to the top and her American dream of working as an engineer were becoming a reality.

On June 1, 1993, NASA sent out an announcement saying it was looking for new astronauts. Kalpana had her application ready to go, and she sent it in. A whole year went by, but she didn't give up hope. She persisted, letting NASA know when she earned new pilot qualifications and when she published papers about her scientific work. Then Kalpana got some exciting news: she was invited to go to the Johnson Space Center in Houston for interviews!

Lots of people interviewed Kalpana when she got to Houston, including some of the astronauts who were working with NASA at the time. She also had to be checked out by doctors, pass a physical fitness test, and be observed in social settings. The medical exams were so thorough, the doctor knew she was a vegetarian even without her telling them! After that, the FBI had to run a background check and talk to people who knew her so they

could learn more about who she was as a person.

Jean-Pierre was in Kentucky when he heard the news. Kalpana's father read it on the front page of a newspaper in New Delhi. In December

1994, after years of hard work and perseverance, Kalpana Chawla got the call that would change her life and the world: she had been accepted into the NASA Astronaut Corps! Out of over four thousand applicants, only nineteen people had made the cut. Kalpana was one of them. Her dreams had officially taken flight. It was now time to move back to Texas so she could reach the stars.

# CHAPTER 4

# Columbia Dreams

A stronaut training was tough, but Kalpana never backed down from a challenge. To be an astronaut, you have to be in excellent physical health. Kalpana started exercising daily, sometimes at the astronaut gym, other times going for a jog at the Johnson Space Center. She trained in parachute jumping and outdoor survival skills on both land and water. Once, when she was doing part of her training in Florida, she even hiked in the jungle and lived off the land for a few days. She also had ejection-seat training. For that, Kalpana was belted into a seat that slid down a rail into a swimming pool, and the seat was then tipped upside down while she was underwater. Kalpana had to remain calm, unbuckle herself, and get to the surface. But the hard work didn't bother Kalpana. "Going to work is so much fun," she once said after a particularly long day. Kalpana was living her passion, and she loved it.

It's a NASA tradition that new astronaut groups get a nickname from the previous ones. Kalpana's group was called the Slugs and the Flying Escargots. Kalpana also chose a new nickname for herself. Since some people at NASA had unfortunately not been pronouncing her name properly, she decided to go by her initials, K. C.

In the fall of 1996, Kalpana was chosen to join the *Columbia* crew. Out of the seven astronauts, she was the only woman chosen for this mission. The crew arrived at Kennedy Space Center in Florida on November 16, 1997. She invited a few guests to watch her launch, and over the next couple of days, her parents, friends, and former professors started arriving. There were so many people who had supported her along the way, and no one wanted to miss the chance to see Kalpana blast off, closer than ever to touching the stars she had admired as a little girl in Karnal.

Astronauts are allowed to bring personal items with them on missions, and Kalpana packed pins to give to friends and family when she returned so that they could have something from her time in space. She also packed a photo of

J. R. D. Tata, India's first licensed pilot and the founder of Air India; a University of Colorado medallion; an Indian Airlines flag; and T-shirts from the Abhinaya School of Dance, the Tagore Baal Niketan School, and the University of Texas at Arlington, among other things. Many of the items had to do with other people: they were objects that made her think back on the incredible journey she had taken. Kalpana was aware of the many people and institutions that had helped reach this point.

*Columbia* lifted off at 2:46 p.m. on November 19, 1997. It made 252 orbits around Earth in just two weeks. Kalpana later said that when the astronauts fired the orbital maneuvering systems, which controlled the shuttle's orbit, it sounded like cannon fire. On her first day in orbit, she said she felt like she was falling forward—there was no gravity in space, and that took some getting used to! She even had trouble sleeping, probably because she was so excited.

"One of the strangest things is that when I was about to sleep, I realized I was only aware of my thoughts. Because you are weightless, you don't feel your legs or your body," she said afterward. "In a sense then, you are just your intelligence. It's amazing, you can't feel anything but your consciousness."

*Columbia's* mission was to send a new satellite, called Spartan, to study the outer layer of the sun. As a mission specialist, Kalpana's job was to operate the robotic arm that would release the satellite. When that time came, though, Kalpana had a problem. As hard as she tried, she couldn't get

the satellite to respond the way she needed it to.
Two other crew members had to do a space walk
to get the satellite back. Though some people said
that Kalpana had made a mistake in her work, she
persisted, confident in herself and her abilities.

Later, after an investigation, NASA learned that it wasn't Kalpana's error that caused the problem. She had not made any mistakes. Sometimes, things don't work out exactly as we plan. But that doesn't mean we quit. Kalpana certainly didn't.

Kalpana landed back on Earth safely and reunited with friends and family. She had made history on the *Columbia* mission as the first Indian woman and first Indian American woman to go to space.

· · · · · · · · · · · · · · · · · · · · · · · · · · ·

## Space Dreams

B eing home on Earth was fun, but Kalpana hoped she would get a chance to go back to space. And during the summer of 2000, her wish came true. She was selected to join the crew of another Columbia mission, along with astronauts Rick Husband, Mike Anderson, Willie McCool, Dave Brown, Laurel Clark, and Ilan Ramon. She was thrilled to get the chance to touch the stars again.

Kalpana prepared carefully for her next trip
to space. As part of the wake-up ritual on the
shuttle, astronauts get to pick music that will be
played during the mission. On her first mission,
Kalpana had chosen sitar music by Ravi Shankar,

a famed Indian musician. For this trip, she chose a song by Abida Parveen, a celebrated Pakistani musician. Even soaring high, Kalpana's roots were strong.

Her personal preference kit, like on her first mission, contained lots of items that reminded her of friends and family: a DAV College for Women patch; the patches of schools her husband attended; a University of Texas at Arlington T-shirt; flags of the National Science Museum and Nehru Planetarium in New Delhi; a Punjab Engineering College banner; and a city of Karnal flag, among other things. She even flew with a copy of *Song for the Blue Ocean* by Carl Safina, a book she enjoyed.

She also studied hard for the mission itself. She reviewed space shuttle manuals, making sure to clarify how things were supposed to happen. Her notes were so good that many astronauts after her used them as part of their learning and preparation.

After some delays, the *Columbia* mission was scheduled to leave on January 16, 2003. This was her beloved niece Neha's birthday. So as a surprise for Neha, Kalpana had arranged for the crowd gathered in the stands to watch the shuttle launch, to sing "Happy Birthday." Kalpana was ready to make history again, and her friends, family, and so many fans were there to cheer her on. It was a safe, successful takeoff. Her family watched NASA TV often, so they were up-to-date on their beloved Kalpana.

Kalpana loved observing Earth from space. "The earth is not just a bluish hue. You actually see all the colors. It was spectacular. For example, when the Sahara comes into view, the ocean near it is an emerald green. It is shockingly beautiful," Kalpana said.

Videoconferencing from the shuttle was always a highlight. Kalpana would get on the camera and talk to her family on Earth, showing off funny tricks that could only be done without gravity, like tumbles and catching floating food in her mouth.

Sixteen days passed, and after a successful mission in the cosmos, it was time for *Columbia* to come back home. But February 1, 2003, was a very sad day.

As the *Columbia* shuttle reentered Earth's atmosphere, tragedy struck, and the shuttle broke apart. All the astronauts on board, including

Kalpana, died that day. The accident shook the world, which mourned alongside the astronauts' families and friends for those who had perished. The astronauts had lost their lives chasing their dreams—and along the way, they had helped make discoveries that would change the future.

## Kalpana's Legacy

In the days after the accident, thousands of volunteers helped to recover what they could. Two official members of the recovery team, Jules F. Mier and Charles Krenek, also lost their lives during the Columbia recovery mission. Kalpana's family received an outpouring of love and support from people all over the world. In accordance with her wishes, they cremated her body. Kalpana was cremated in her blue NASA flight suit, which contained notes from her loved ones. Her ashes were scattered in Utah, in Zion National Park, a place she loved. Kalpana was gone from Earth, but her memory and contributions still inspire so many people today.

Her dad visited her office after the accident. He wanted to see her desk. He was touched to find a photo of their family, along with her collection of neatly lined-up toy planes, at her workspace. "Just listen to your daughters, listen to what they have to say. They want to study, let them," he said. "Support them. Make sure they have all that they need to simply focus on their education."

Kalpana loved aviation and she loved her family. She loved space travel and science. She was a unique, hardworking woman who knew that girls could achieve anything they wanted,

even if some people didn't think so at the time.

Kalpana was awarded many medals and honors after she died. Her family accepted the NASA Space Flight Medal and the NASA Distinguished Service Medal on her behalf. She was also awarded the Congressional Space Medal of Honor. In 2003, Indian Prime Minister Atal Bihari Vajpayee announced that India's series of weather satellites would be named Kalpana.

Kalpana's name is also on buildings and celestial bodies. There's an asteroid named after her and all the other crew members of the Columbia mission. And the girls' dorm at Punjab Engineering College, where Kalpana went to college when there was no girls' dorm at all, is named after her as well. In Queens, New York, in the heavily South Asian neighborhood of Jackson Heights, 74th Street is now called Kalpana Chawla Way. And there's a medical college and hospital in Karnal, a dorm at the University of Texas at Arlington, and a hill on Mars named after her, too.

At the Kennedy Space Center in Florida, there's a memorial to Kalpana and all the other *Columbia* crew members who lost their lives. Kalpana's memorial includes her favorite book,

*Jonathan Livingston Seagull* by Richard Bach, as well as a model glider airplane, a bird feeder to honor her love of bird-watching, and binoculars to represent her deep passion for observing nature.

More than anything, Kalpana was remembered for her love of flying and for being a smart, wonderful friend. "Kalpana, or K. C. to her friends, was admired personally for her extraordinary kindness and technically for her strive for perfection," said Kent Rominger, who worked with her at NASA. "She had a terrific sense of humor, loved flying small airplanes with her husband and loved flying in space. Flying was her passion. She would often remind her crew as her training flow would be delayed and become extended, she would say, 'Man, you are training to fly in space. What more could you want?' "

Kalpana Chawla was the first American astronaut of Indian origin to go to space. And her dreams, born in Karnal, blossomed in America. She was determined to achieve her goals, and when she succeeded, she set new, tougher goals for herself. She was an astronaut, a daughter, a sister, an aunt, a friend, a scientist, an immigrant, a bird-watcher, a nature lover, a pilot, and a reader. She was a bright star.

Kalpana persisted, even when things seemed impossible. And no matter what your dream is, you can persist, too.

# HOW YOU CAN PERSIST

by Raakhee Mirchandani

If you want to honor Kalpana's memory, pursue your passions, and learn more about our planet and galaxy, there's so much you can do. Like Kalpana, you have the power to break barriers. Here's how to get started:

1. Be a feminist. Being a feminist means you support equal rights for girls and women.

2. Try something new. Try something challenging. If there's a new hobby you're thinking of trying, tell a friend and do it together. Learning new things isn't just fun, it's good for your brain!

3. Take a hike. Grab some binoculars and take a trip around your neighborhood or on a trail. See how many animals and birds you can spot. Appreciate the nature around you.

4. Recycle. We only have one planet and it's our responsibility to care for it.

5. Listen to songs in another language or music from a different culture, like the astronauts did on the *Columbia* missions.

6. Visit a planetarium or a museum and learn more about our solar system.

7. Talk about Kalpana. Do a school project about her and tell others about her incredible life.

8. Learn about the contributions of immigrants and immigrant communities in America. And while you're at it, share these accomplishments with others.

9. Wish upon a star. When you see a star twinkling in the night sky, think about Kalpana and make a wish for yourself or for someone you love.

10. Pronounce people's names correctly. And pronounce your own name the way it is meant to be said, not in a way

that makes it "easier" for others to say. Names are sacred and important, and making an effort to learn how to say someone's name is kind and respectful.

11. Don't take no for an answer. You can be anything you want; don't let anyone tell you otherwise. You got this!

# ACKNOWLEDGMENTS

I have admired Kalpana Chawla since I was a teen-
ager. Her passion, purpose, and drive have profoundly
impacted my life. And when my daughter, Satya, was
just a toddler, I hung a photo of Kalpana in her room so
she knew, like our hero, anything was possible for her,
too, with hard work, persistence, and an open heart. I
am grateful for this opportunity to preserve her legacy
and share her story with a new generation of young
readers and leaders. I am especially grateful to my agent,
Liza Fleissig, for championing me and encouraging me to
tell Kalpana's story. Your support is empowering. Thank
you to the brilliant editorial team of Jill Santopolo and
Talia Benamy at Penguin Random House—you both are
changing bookshelves and the world. Thank you for wel-
coming me to the #Persisterhood with enthusiasm and
friendship. And to the entire Philomel team, including
Alexandra Boiger, Gillian Flint, Ellice Lee, Lori Thorn,
Laura Davis, and Krista Ahlberg, thank you for treating

Kalpana's story with such grace. A heartfelt thanks to Chelsea Clinton for making this space; the She Persisted series is a celebration of sisterhood for readers of all ages and genders. I am so proud to be part of the club. And please also thank your mom for me; when I give Satya examples of women who persist, she is always at the top of my list.

I also wanted to acknowledge Kalpana's family. Losing a loved one is incredibly difficult, and I hold you all tightly in my heart. I read what you wrote about her and listened to the interviews you gave in the months and years after the tragedy. Your love for her—and each other—is so strong. This book is an offering to all of you, written by someone who admires her so deeply. Your Kalpana's star still burns bright.

Thank you to my parents, Deena and Pirkash and Surjit and Birinder, for all your support as I worked on this story. I especially want to thank Dad for proofreading my pages and giving me feedback. As a working parent, I know that partnership and community are the reasons

I am able to chase my own dreams. Agan, together, we can do anything. And to my incredible mom squad: Elidia Aponte, Neve Kondili, Jennifer Parikh, Jessica Kechian, Kat Blostein, and Hema Pyarilal, thank you for caring for Satya like she was your own as I researched and wrote this book. Supriya Kelkar, my writing partner and book sister, and Mrs. Markowitz, my high school English teacher and friend, thanks for always cheering me along.

To my daughter, Satya, this world isn't just yours, it's yours to make better. Make space for others, use your voice, and listen when others use theirs. And like our hero Kalpana, never stop reaching for the stars.

# ᔕ References ᔐ

Belluck, Pam. "Loss of the Shuttle: The
Astronauts; The Columbia Space Shuttle's
Crew of 6 Americans and 1 Israeli." *The
New York Times*, February 2, 2003. nytimes
.com/2003/02/02/us/loss-shuttle-astronauts
-columbia-space-shuttle-s-crew-6-americans
-1-israeli-146404.html.

"Biographical Data." Kalpana Chawla, NASA,
    May 2004. nasa.gov/sites/default/files/atoms
    /files/chawla_kalpana.pdf.

Brut India. "The Life of Astronaut Kalpana
    Chawla." February 14, 2021. Educational
    video, 5:02. youtube.com/watch?v=14fXq
    -2gSAE.

Chengappa, Raj. "I Really Feel Responsible
    for the Earth Now: Kalpana Chawla." *India
    Today*, January 26, 1998. indiatoday.in
    /magazine/interview/story/19980126-i-really
    -feel-responsible-for-the-earth-now-says-kalpana
    -chawla-825487-1998-01-26.

Harrison, Jean-Pierre. *The Edge of Time*. Los
Gatos: Harrison Publishing, 2011.

Harvey, Alisa and Nola Taylor Tillman.
"Kalpana Chawla: Biography & Columbia
Disaster." Space.com, February 10, 2022.
space.com/17056-kalpana-chawla-biography
.html.

Kalpana Chawla Memorial Display, University
of Texas at Arlington. uta.edu/academics
/schools-colleges/engineering/about/facilities
/kc-exhibit.

"Kalpana Chawla Said, Someday She'd Be
'Kidnapped' in Outer Space: Father."

NDTV.com, October 24, 2019. ndtv.com
/india-news/kalpana-chawla-said-someday
-shed-be-kidnapped-in-outer-space-father
-banarasi-lal-chawla-2121982.

*Mega Icons.* 2020. Season 2, Episode 4, "Kalpana
Chawla." National Geographic (India).

Mukherjee, Jashodhara. "17 Years After Kalpana
Chawla's Death," Her Father Opens Up
About Her Dream. *News18*, October 11, 2020.
news18.com/news/buzz/17-years-after-kalpana
-chawlas-death-her-father-opens-up-about-her
-dream-2941149.html.

RAAKHEE MIRCHANDANI is a children's book author, activist, and mama—not necessarily in that order. The New Jersey–born daughter of Indian immigrants, Raakhee is a proud supporter of many nonprofits, serving on the boards of the Hoboken Public Library, Stevens Cooperative School, and Drag Queen Story Hour NYC. When she is not reading or writing, Raakhee can be found organizing her bookshelves or drinking coffee at the many adorable coffee shops in Hoboken, New Jersey, where she lives with her husband, Agan, and daughter, Satya.

Photo credit: Kim Lorraine Photography

You can visit Raakhee Mirchandani online at
RaakstarWrites.com
or follow her on Twitter
@Raakstar
and on Instagram
@RaakstarWrites

GILLIAN FLINT has worked as a professional illustrator since earning an animation and illustration degree in 2003. Her work has since been published in the UK, USA and Australia. In her spare time, Gillian enjoys reading, spending time with her family and puttering about in the garden on sunny days. She lives in the northwest of England.

*Courtesy of the illustrator*

You can visit Gillian Flint online at
gillianflint.com
or follow her on Twitter
@GillianFlint
and on Instagram
@gillianflint_illustration

CHELSEA CLINTON is the author of the #1 *New York Times* bestseller *She Persisted: 13 American Women Who Changed the World*; *She Persisted Around the World: 13 Women Who Changed History*; *She Persisted in Sports: American Olympians Who Changed the Game*; *Don't Let Them Disappear: 12 Endangered Species Across the Globe*; *It's Your World: Get Informed, Get Inspired & Get Going!*; *Start Now!: You Can Make a Difference*; with Hillary Clinton, *Grandma's Gardens* and *Gutsy Women*; and, with Devi Sridhar, *Governing Global Health: Who Runs the World and Why?* She is also the Vice Chair of the Clinton Foundation, where she works on many initiatives, including those that help empower the next generation of leaders. She lives in New York City with her husband, Marc, their children and their dog, Soren.

You can follow Chelsea Clinton on Twitter
@ChelseaClinton
or on Facebook at
facebook.com/chelseaclinton

ALEXANDRA BOIGER has illustrated nearly twenty picture books, including the She Persisted books by Chelsea Clinton; the popular Tallulah series by Marilyn Singer; and the Max and Marla books, which she also wrote. Originally from Munich, Germany, she now lives outside of San Francisco, California, with her husband, Andrea, daughter, Vanessa, and two cats, Luiso and Winter.

You can visit Alexandra Boiger online at
alexandraboiger.com
or follow her on Instagram
@alexandra_boiger

# Read about more inspiring women in the

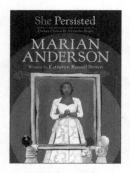

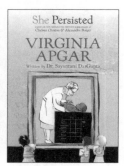

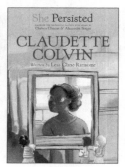

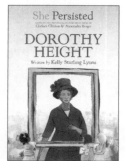

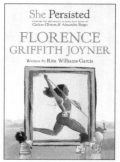

# She Persisted series!

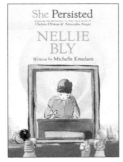

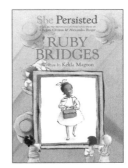

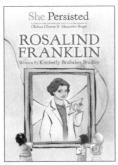

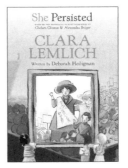

**She Persisted**
BASED ON THE BESTSELLING PICTURE BOOK SERIES BY
Chelsea Clinton & Alexandra Boiger
**RACHEL LEVINE**
Written by Lisa Bunker

**She Persisted**
BASED ON THE BESTSELLING PICTURE BOOK SERIES BY
Chelsea Clinton & Alexandra Boiger
**MAYA LIN**
Written by Grace Lin

**She Persisted**
BASED ON THE BESTSELLING PICTURE BOOK SERIES BY
Chelsea Clinton & Alexandra Boiger
**WANGARI MAATHAI**
Written by Eucabeth Odhiambo

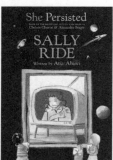

**She Persisted**
BASED ON THE BESTSELLING PICTURE BOOK SERIES BY
Chelsea Clinton & Alexandra Boiger
**SALLY RIDE**
Written by Atia Abawi

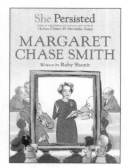

**She Persisted**
BASED ON THE BESTSELLING PICTURE BOOK SERIES BY
Chelsea Clinton & Alexandra Boiger
**MARGARET CHASE SMITH**
Written by Ruby Shamir

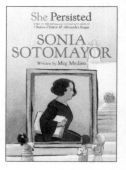

**She Persisted**
BASED ON THE BESTSELLING PICTURE BOOK SERIES BY
Chelsea Clinton & Alexandra Boiger
**SONIA SOTOMAYOR**
Written by Meg Medina

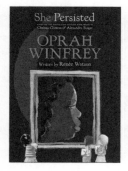

**She Persisted**
BASED ON THE BESTSELLING PICTURE BOOK SERIES BY
Chelsea Clinton & Alexandra Boiger
**OPRAH WINFREY**
Written by Renée Watson

**She Persisted**
BASED ON THE BESTSELLING PICTURE BOOK SERIES BY
Chelsea Clinton & Alexandra Boiger
**MALALA YOUSAFZAI**
Written by Aisha Saeed

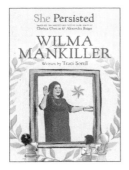

She Persisted
BASED ON THE BESTSELLING PICTURE BOOK INSPIRED BY
Chelsea Clinton & Alexandra Boiger
WILMA
MANKILLER
Written by Traci Sorell

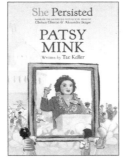

She Persisted
BASED ON THE BESTSELLING PICTURE BOOK INSPIRED BY
Chelsea Clinton & Alexandra Boiger
PATSY
MINK
Written by Tae Keller

She Persisted
BASED ON THE BESTSELLING PICTURE BOOK INSPIRED BY
Chelsea Clinton & Alexandra Boiger
FLORENCE
NIGHTINGALE
Written by Shelli R. Johannes

She Persisted
BASED ON THE BESTSELLING PICTURE BOOK INSPIRED BY
Chelsea Clinton & Alexandra Boiger
MARIA
TALLCHIEF
Written by Christine Day

She Persisted
BASED ON THE BESTSELLING PICTURE BOOK INSPIRED BY
Chelsea Clinton & Alexandra Boiger
DIANA
TAURASI
Written by Monica Brown

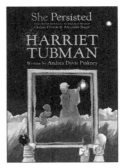

She Persisted
BASED ON THE BESTSELLING PICTURE BOOK INSPIRED BY
Chelsea Clinton & Alexandra Boiger
HARRIET
TUBMAN
Written by Andrea Davis Pinkney